never
have a bad day
ever again

never
have a bad day
ever again

max wigram and murray partridge

quadrille

It's now official. reports have finally started to prove what we all knew all along: that it's the little things in life that make us happy.

This book lists nearly a hundred of those little things. simple, daily pleasures that cost nothing and that can really make a difference.

Try a few, or all, of them.

Start now, enjoy these little pleasures, take a moment to savour them, and you may find that you'll never have a truly bad day ever again.

rubbing your face, head and ears hard

tearing up junk mail

thinking of somebody fatter than you

writing a love letter to yourself

dancing

leaning against the wind

talking about something and then not doing it

talking about something and then doing it

turning off the telly

flirting

leaving the washing up

sending someone flowers for no reason

farting

sneezing and farting at the same time (snarting)

popping bubblewrap

writing something with a fountain pen

sticking your head out of the window

when it's raining

enjoying a good word
(like 'bell-end' or 'pungent')

saying 'oof' as you slump into a chair

shutting up and listening

putting on a hat

peeing after holding it in

letting somebody else take the credit

when everyone knows it was you

a good stretch

a siesta

a good wank

second gear

a clean shirt

a good shit

talking to someone who's listening

realising you don't actually need that much

taking a deep breath

screaming

revving up next to a guy at the lights,

then letting him race off first

fondling your own buttocks

not bothering to judge people

finding a ripe avocado

boasting

winning an argument in your head

reading about celebrities

who've fucked up their lives

phoning a helpline and shouting 'help'!

learning a few words of Swahili

singing

laughing

fucking

letting someone believe what they want

skiving

lying down and relaxing your arsehole

getting rid of stuff

thinking about past shags

thinking about future shags

toupee spotting

being nice unnecessarily

letting someone else fix global warming

eavesdropping

thinking about killing someone you hate

telling your old stories to someone new

gently holding someone's gaze

farting with a hard-on

(men only – called woodwind)

crawling around on all fours barking

waiting for the facts

writing the first paragraph of a novel

and not bothering with the rest

thinking about someone fancying you

fancying yourself

being humble but still getting all the credit

letting go to get a better hold

being the calm one

being even ruder to somebody rude

playing air guitar

giving the impression that you are more
successful than you are without actually lying

kicking dry leaves

telling someone a secret

changing the subject when

somebody starts talking about house prices

avoiding a boring or difficult phone
conversation by leaving a voicemail instead

making up a new swear word

(like arsecunt or dogwank)

rejoicing that you're not in hospital

rejoicing that you never went into politics

thinking about phoning somebody,

then not bothering

outliving someone nasty

making an old person happy just by saying hello

squeezing a spot

smelling the flowers

cheating the taxman

turning off your cell phone

using anything with wheels

whistling

changing your mind

setting your sights low

watching an expert

porn

a good spoonerism

the dawn chorus

If you can think of any delicious, little, everyday pleasures
that we have missed, please post them on our website
www.neverhaveabadday.com

First published in 2008 by
Quadrille Publishing Limited
Alhambra House
27-31 Charing Cross Road
London WC2H 0LS

Cataloguing in Publication Data: a catalogue record for this book is
available from the British Library

ISBN 978 184400 626 7 (Charcoal)
ISBN 978 184400 657 1 (Pink)

Printed and bound in China